I lay too many Eggs in the hot Sands of this Wilderness, the World! with Ostrich Carelessness & Ostrich Oblivion.

S.T. Coleridge, *Biographia Literaria*

Yeah, it's the old one; I wrote this about probably fourteen years ago or so; I don't know which wrecked car of Pat's it was before.

Blaze Foley, his live intro to *Cold, Cold World*

in grateful acknowledgment to these journals' editors, where these poems, sometimes in slightly different shapes, first appeared

Phoebe - 5, 8, 10, 23, 44, 45, 62

Salt Hill - 9, 11, & epilogue

Denver Quarterly - 31

Dusie - excerpt from 'adult compost'

jubilat - 12 & prologue

CutBank - 19 & 42

The Bakery - 37, 38, 39, 40, 41, 52, 53, 55, 57

Pinwheel - 2, 22, 34, 49

Bayou Magazine - 18, 26, 59

Ghost Proposal - 4, 13, 27, 58

Columbia Poetry Review - 48, 51, 54

The Pinch - 35

only jesus could icefish in summer

abraham smith

for linda detra

prologue

only two kinds of people gone
icefishing and we
we were never the shanty caliber typo
somebody almost dramatic drunk hit the A chord
with a tremolo flourish err finish
as though there's an audience
beyond a starved herd of birches begging you
not to call 'em bandaged bones no it was sit
sit sit sit sit on a flipped five gallon bucket
mmm and the bucket was green as spring
on a shirt advertising summer
dreamed by a kid with a cow called sugar
and the bell round the neck sings
all sounds clept cept shirked
over a hole drilled by going crazy circular
by hand by men going out there you got fast
that that car was fast
would not fast for gas
was unholy drinking in
they were sharing a bottle
up at the beach err bench front seat
and the sound of that
was a creek one day's like screw it
i am gonna drink myself
and the color of the backseat
i sat alone in
was not what it was
given light's feather teeth
all over half the passage of time
maybe mushroom gill spit spill get brown
g chord the thing twists out of
the serial killer's slag heap grasp
'mon let's rowdy earnest folkie timber nowsville

so the right the car sounds
like a bog swallowing thunderstorms' saws
and bombs eons of their little whirring teeth
and spam until a priest picking ferns
lady's slipper wintergreen leather leaf
punctures the peat for one long
one long roar
and the color of the hole they'd spun
was that same black of the priest heeled booo
and grrr and the color of the sky above
while we fished of aspirin and of tin
and the lake ice all the time moaning
for it loved itself for it was a smug lake
named by squintin trappers err
for beards of venison smoke and venery err
for beards of taters' prism blighty err for beards
of bluegills' perfect milk bath flesh
grayed of worm inn maybe
and the cold was try and walk off to pee
try and pull your zipper down you'd
easier hold a metal metal metal ladder
weight of ten cow and the five machine
it takes to keep the ten
ladder hold it with your stare
never mind winds to 40
with the bendy paper hands in your weaker eye lad
left with no taste mechanism left
he so breathed the fires of others in
ladder tranced to the cheeks of iced houses skid skids
cold i can't explain but can't keep you
waiting like this so metal
for braces for kids with polio
fettered the air migrates mystery pollen

zero seed broadcast limpet winnow is
super stalker lover sproutless
how was it ever such with leaves??
and now for measure flour measure of lard
as i will tell how i got in
to go home for the orphans are all in
chicago they will tell you i have heard them
trying to know themselves
by way o' suck a thumb
i had to hip it had to body bump the dumb thick union
metal button on the car door to unclick it
were weaker than watching someone walk away to pee
those little fishbone paper fingers of mine
that is all that's it
that and i grow cold easy quick the theory goes
never end on i
so december cat
mazy mow stack
sits top half assed squares
last year's rain sunnings
sits all deeeep in her december bones
she sits she purrs that's the mouse ears rattling
will warm will warn an cubit of you
it's old holed tarps in a wind
work to listen to plastic wounds
our ears will speech like watered shells
where we are going to maybe

small fails

1

it's not that true that ears
are can openers and we cut
the world circle open
according to some universal
prescribed canal ideal
no you can train yourself to hear
the groat of envy fall
on seeming solar ash birds
see all birds are born to a striped logic
a string line of charts and charms
and they are what they are the one they are
by saying same span the span
that's their reach way
fire undresses the world
addresses the lie of the whole
and so if i
if i am thinking one thing
legs bent way we do down a hill
it is what bird is that and what
would i if ever i could cud one thing
if my me were in that one thing forever fadeless
call that what cheese you wish
it matters me a great deal
let this swiss door
sack glass let sound
lie i know no door

2

you pretty much caught me
pouring water in milk
that's like making curtains
out of old negligees folks have not suffered
same with music
when they sang for god
wicked and wonder fill fee
lot to be said for being scared as hell
chin up and
down in a good hole
that aspen crown for a month
in winter with your stethoscope
on a sleeping bear and tell me
that the earth does not go
mighty slow in stretching of midge
into eagle eating crow
i heard a mature eagle tried to take a fawn
the fawn did get up off the ground
a little but it was a no go
because the wings were stupid about fawn
and then the flies
those two fishy talon wounds
for five days by my lights
and i am the only one
on earth with broken booze glass
for eyes closer to water
the more the numberless bitin buzzes
it's yours i won't air colored
garden hose stretching between
up there and this little lost rambler
oh guess it's downhill all

post partial kill sky
knee guess it's knees then nape
in creek with a hey with a croupy wire hanger
of flies all popcorning down
like deer were bouncy wire hanger
we stretched into a basketball hoop
and shut the door and loved
that trim and door
would hold it up there children
maybe expect some fairly crazy things
and rolled dirty socks and dunked
the tastes for running
soon gained weight my one
and only hands

3

darling is regrettable beginning
for iamb as in no olde movie and can't
believe the starlet i ah at
exploded her casket from
the fumes for rotting
if not the sweet ass lie
of earth on earth on earth we'd heard it pop
darn ling melting
old red and yellow blocky phones down now
card an astronaut fire and
pat an astronaut fireman suit
into 2 astronaut scabs
same way kids slap a very not man
of snow we actually
work opposite greater the higher
but why quib there are rules
no earth child plays by in winter
truth there is more down there
than evacuation for example
what i feel
water would not shine without wind
to earthquake the jelly hell out of it
revised revising
the sex the compass
the heart lotus clock galosh
the head this crisp vie 'zine sail
cannot we cannot hear so can't
compare the threat to tear to fire
and peace and white and wide
that's just like you to almost wince
at what might one day be broken

at least poked into
by the barreling marrow pea winds
just like you again
to pinch the insides
of the seed where it roots roosts
roofs so green
sea water the tints of breakfast fruits
sail bullshit motion of no earthly bread
sky this slab of theory water
tang moat truer
the bathroom window say
when the rockstar throws is throwing up elsewhere

4

why stack this
in a neat little pile
on the floor by the records
that you and only you
know how to sing to
having learned all the skips
as little goings quiet and wet
the dust where this was
if you like i
squeamish memory
squeeze hands first into
hearts then potatoes
escape it by a coughing or
any little key caulk jocular song
darling readying the tshirts
sunset jellyroll
correction
ruddy sunrise actually
fact that eyebrow ain't
trough for sojourning monarch
handsome trap
sweat some jelly teeth
crown o' gliding fang
as we yes yes no from
the latest in a clear stretch
before dark woods
dark lite afterthoughts of
explosion wroth
remnant microphone
cords everywhere
retract retrace

is it we are too animal ever to
butter feather into the room
where crooners stare
rare holes in smoke
and red red lips
button nest
little murders
to the edges of glass

in cloven signature stray
come now with a voice
like a coffee table to steer
a picaresque with me
people ask where is
easy fingers on eyelids in dreams
twitch junk hills jump
in wars me i only lonely line difference
between that and heartbeats
bird versus fish
fist verse bomb wind
what ills doll is the fizz
line bobwhite bombin boom
mmm shoulder pain
that's a sweet hurt that's a natural
crank ol loony loomin like a mirror where
the people went home from for the summer caddy
even when there's none past ol factory home
best if we just live in n's and m's
and on and om stuff a clove up there
it's like of cork they they and they
there there and there and it's
six weeks 'fore new years and
everybody's uncareful eight
gone mine by claw and pinchin day
to night it's like they invented a button
to do that pressure on the right
kind of water gone the rite
kind of wrong just in time
to your head i love it
kiss a federal fire disaster site

the jitters yours that
traveling kills what's under
try gurgle well
in every parched dirt part
and leaf that roarin book
try not leaf rash with gloves on
sympathetic blisters yours
yet you never feel free
short of plural of wheel
there so there no there
no there

6

leather weathervane
tip tip smoke to breathe
into a broken pity
pretty cheap heal
heels unwelcome very
except those hoo
who've walked so long
in the garden as to leather
like stone the heel
and by garden a path
and by path i mean a crooked deer
road knows only
head down follow
former way back when
some 2 browned ones watched for trees
or didn't sleeping rope a deer road is

7

let us sudden
sunlight car crash bonnet
my words shitty cereal
all tittle toll in the milk
bowl your bonnet is in sun turn in
wine urn inn let's
all in dare
branching reel

8

these fine five nine cent birds
penny ante we are down
to sparrow today things
could not be finer squats
not blessed with too strong a rope
is blessed depends on your thinking
between eyeball and thinking
pecks up bit spat fingernail quasi
smoking gun clips
yours particularly
that's the world for you
automatic thing
everyday's a trash day
and is on the air
chest out heart ponytail
on a trot isn't it such a thing
that little horned moon
of a nail out from the beak
and bird with branchlet says another world
beyond the water toss
wit nervous tick rent bends
tween highway big spyware
and hope i don't err
in circle's constancy
just rounding now
friend don't
don't crowd
these little stray
infinitesimal breakers of no

9

swoon or bode o both bottle fed
cousins and they don't know it going
to bed in a cart and four
couldn't help it the rattle
gendered by holed
roads shoves they close id
weed sheen shade skit deplorable
hot skin society suck a hell
man that wall is floor able
deuce or nine
the number's naughty knot's juicy sigh
when one's perceptions
persephone percival
of wallowing happen
while wallowing
in a cattle tank bath
is it mermaid moccasin gin it is
win win win win win win win

10

other tweeter missed bit clips humped up
by ant if mouth in back
as upon the aegis-like body
if the deflection of a touch
is a declension's wreck then
something like my sword
borne mm windmill's monster
arms unmonster deeper
than the dead waters
surface is usable friend
up here all friend

11

i can say the bog bark same
my emotions happened much
in feathers
and flowers kicked by
hotties in hip hugger denim now now's the time
to kick the roof off my pillow
stuffers in suction boots standing by
their sack cloth trailing light
in breeze
like milk could die
and have a second mother light too

12

we live in space i mean
are on like tv to the lonely until wear
the sound of all cars going
in one paper-tooth saw-unlike sauna
on high on cold and then
the crows we live with
is to say they signal our sentience
reach off off the pines
highway or any little dirt road
mmm hums like polished glass or
anxious owned caves and the crows
and then the crows clown
like dog ears at a listening
and seeing and runnin trot i mean
the trot and ear are flop complicated
like three mice pulling on a
so not one for all crumb
see there's more than sit to butts
let's just say the neck that tower
of words or no words
don't house kapow
ain't as rarified as the steak
all plumber snake naked
in the lobbyists' gulleted claims
cry blood pipe
that crumb needs a hot therapist
it's free to hear helpless
in the unlocked scratchings
of claws on no hold good wood rafters
burned right
up to the edges of hardness and the crows

their callings more like a thing torn
from a thing than carefully lathed
administers of keys of cheese
orgy gone viral on palmed phones
impeach all idle wankers yes the crow
with a bas haw baa maybe
marbles heaven maybe try liking
burn wounds healed

13

the crows are i am home
as in i go to the rib doctor
in taos tell him pull one
i go to the duck decoy doctor
with that no laugh
or deep breath for at
least six weeks rib north of
minneapolis tell her
whittle me a wind wanderer
i go to the glassblower md
boston by way of fayetteville
tell him blow me a dip vessel
bout the size of the pineal and i
go to the big printer makers
before you homogenize the inks
in them big expense cubes i am as in
an animal under the leaves
am the leaves for all the eye
and the leaves ain't worth
thinking about since milton so
mind if i siphon a bag of
your rawest finest so
so home in crow as in yard chicken
eggs for breakfast
them yokes blood orange
they candle the heart
them kids five things
before the noon winter sun like a white nail
before breakfast even
lamb duck mama to plastic waa waa lion train

14

careful not
to careful the kid out
of the kid try couple
of ladysmith's finest
blackest smartest
phone back when you had to set it down
to hang up on the chaperones
of these couple years
worth of caws sans malfeasance hang up on
the pines and spiral out gentle
as blood clot bound for brain? naw
as what would kid said
i have no jelly bracelet
listen clicking knee back before it clicked
licorice ranger rick rickets
isn't anything want to come back from
back when mead meant
paper wasn't loopy honey
mercy that old boat of a car
the tailpipe pipe vibrates
the leaves of the forget
the names of the trees
waggle like high school
cabaret dance happy hands
done under water
think no drowning
mercury make out with lead
licorice pretty oil war
belt buckle what a
rocky bottom beach nuisance

cun-click it come hear sandy
under water wader on the mind
eye wood haft hat husky varnish sic

15

does not ardor dog
does beat with yours pure
two too soft bob tank apples
the hairs shook absenting
everything from a fleeing
tax o' dermal deer
slim leaf rock boat loll
light grows old
so charged with milk so breakable
gun powder water
tank was a bucket on the second storey thank you
some things you don't touch water
cares
for you
those old plastic sack apples
psalm solo on the slip knot too

too old to register in the historical
doggerel noses of june
two things the june grass
heads out and the turtles
rise from the wet
just as mechanical
and or dopey romantical
as wood studied by j muir
he believed you want to get
big of leg spirit
find a boulder and jump
on it ahh mmm pay shins
the dud sweet nest
of all first things and on
to the edges of gravel
roads gravel sands
familiar sword first parry
fucked floor shore
and the truck wheel
stones sand you know
jiggles figures
in the gathering shelled
harder of a day turtle
if you remember
one thing turtle begun
and or turtle after it is not
mr farmer trucker stuffed with
number pain til 5 somewhere
but tar wheel tar night
butter sue lazy scars fit
coolly in there somewhere

sounds good it sounds
light it could lean not fall
blubbery elbow dimple works
part time third shift a lot of other
place than face all night alright

17

rain loin enthusiast
burr oak on the door
knock knock with your head
on the door light child in the skins
of the mother kick
kicks and the drunk
cat catches
that hoof to the chest
satchel for your cover late lately for school
pulse wool mood drink dream
sits back
stead of snaps baa to sitting

18

ha stealing try that meal that milk again
star ooze blooming in his mill poke head
star like a froze egg
finally got the balls
for roll all that star dust does
is drop hatch two and track them
down over his eyes all he sees with now
right ear potato geode core
mmm as he proceeds
sideways through the leaves
play at fire change fair
towards the river at night long
long time before dawn says there is
a river

19

what kept me
from shooting myself
when i was ten
was going to the river bridge
fish like flags that's all
all i have ever had
to say
fish like flags and i probably stolid
that from v woolf
sometimes comfortable
with the current sometimes advancing on it
like life

20

we want the dog
for scarp
that it is signaled
and we do not scrape our knees
and the bees do not
assert themselves about the
flowers of our knees clerkin
at the cork factory again
when the man walks in
smoking orphan toe you're fine
ghost of off gravy out the double barrel nostril
someone lifted his arm hairs with the brisks
freaks of her grey pant suit passing
city robot antsy coats don't lie
frame the flood or curbed hollow he has the need
set folks free
from the guilts of proximity
what's on sale sinks around here?
reader let me spill a bean
feared by horses a jumpin bean
on your zit
for as i spun to survey
our fleet of nincompoop radishes
i prayed to jesus's loathsome soggy moonboots
if they if they would drown him
in their blue neck fat and
out of this world

always wanted to
do one like a math therefore
a bird's a food you just
built too many tables
and chairs and chairs on
buses to need that
know how how about
when the world was new
and the only road was
smoke in the air
how it ate itself or else the wind
would not suffer a way
out of here my eye pony lonely
pony belly lonely as a pony
tossed musty pelty hay
pre parade pomp route staged
in a mall parking lot
pretty new redo so there's only one crack
and from that grandma spine tempter
uno regal weed spurts and fakes
i am sorry bowing like the king's
mistress to the king after
she's had hand in juice breaks from things
the pony's just after the mayor
and the mayor has been advised
to chew cinnamon gum
he looks a little bewilderingly
at old farmer face like a bedpost
kid playing jail had notched with days since six
now he's sixteen see the pony's

water closet is the world
my good my good eyes gone traveling
gonna mail them to you to you
send back when can refresh wonder
only every few word-lent bleat-blinks
please won't feel a thing
but back in ooh what's the sound of vision's chestnuts
reclaimed? queequeg? the gin
and the ginned animal
the parable of footy cat off for free
the solo eros arose therefore
we learn to waltz gnawed off
kerplop on three on three
whether we know or no
on three

any place you stood in clear
a boat sailed the ocean
on the timber from there
a view another way of saying a boat
and lonely people peeping
through skinned glint sea
with the bad bread black teeth
the people of bread jawing bread so they
chewed themselves quiet up
so a see going meant a sea going
see mint sea inn endland
was only in the unglassed woods
that leaden footedness trucked with wings
distance's magics consumed
great fat toads name of root and stagger ray
the captain he said he could take the wrinkle
off the ocean if he pulled a string
through one nostril out the other
that would do it
rake the wrinkle right off the ocean
one infinite harsh eye pane
day they switched up tooths for seers
yes he knew that one thing like a call
the viburnum the handful of soil
all the way through himself like sugar
through cake
all you can ask of anybody
convict and crate and cranes the cop
in there that way but don't see him so
he stows fine to a new land
has him a new name

rhymes with fin subsumed in rain
we sleep sleep
re-wets our eyes for
meteor care of crater
yes effin sir
not everything shoulder
wearying chop and
chipping dig

23

a bird a star
a burr a bar or two
a borne sense
rest says
a pine
needle in the wind
the foreboding link forbidden
so unlike rim berm
like the rhythm when one is working well
one has a song in one's head
one's hips move mountains
one's fingers iconoclast
all the ore back in the headless hill
blink to wet the centered next
rolls the bird in yonder egg
will be the vertigo bird
only one with sense of spin
through whippy lippy dark
the stars put themselves out
they rake themselves through
little trees more like shrugging
in a wind shrubs of water up there somewhere
or on us
unknowingly
we what so coolly
their jaws of fish spit cut fire
specious fire
hand hand
when land goes water boys
and all the girls taste of envelope

oh man old man lives
tender as cutting and gutting a fish
with the laughin spoonbill water bill boys
cane me
gonna cane me my way with a gill

your every simile mussed
chops heads o ho
ah ha the mussels
in the rivers abiding
open and close
so eerily put it on a kid show
put a treasure in
put a fry in a face your ever
seam leak offs kings' heads
wides eyes
won't wow awe long
hmm hmm when sky's an examination
room drawer full of boiled tools
and all the world's
to the health of the bird

25

nowhere a garden
mole with passage just for me
lake you twice everything
water that is
that's your magical sit
suet what do you see in me? goat
i aim nimble or these are nails

as to be caught in
a dirty little romance
with a day old fry pan
sick slick cold you cooked once
the white seams of a heart
are not meat to keep the hard ledge
rattling flattening happening time man it was
it was as in get that water mirror shine off
your forward momentum as in parsing
fisted mist with a rain rot
decalogue you mustard oil use your musty
roll and dial rudolph
through the needy
there musts be
something other than
other than muscle and bone
there is a
child with a bowl
just a little country bowl
of ash mother
thumbs her mouth
and into the ash
now onto his nose
bear bear in his eyes
bolds and shies
sleep under earth
in a hole they clawed themselves their hearts almost
stop every year they hear the earth's heart going
when they are walking they are miming the earth
blood caught between laugh cough
a palpitation at the phrase

a year she told he was
honey bear just by just
that one mouth damp driven dot
and roamed and roared for
awhile for a thousand he

i thank god for the limits to my nose
for the dumbing of the breeze
will the road to the sleeper
seeks it clean
rotten ruby ring was a wire talk
do you wear that
to your mouth for a wound or is there
some current thing the smaller
the tighter the turn of the trapped
so fat with rinse
as to be shiny glad? in their clocking
tell you what
stone bend road
pretty lie of a row this way
that ice needs stoves
you could eat off
the pasture weeds and play
you were captain of the cod
none in the cloud kit stupid
no one poisoned the whey
the storm pork wasn't gypsum
for factory belly scratch scrap
frap pistol pop off all y'all
out of my apple trees
you got the milk from my daisy
you don't need god telling me
i got a sweetheart
in indy and her too

love is a dream
today fine treasure
you get your pick of after
they've cleaned your teeth up and sewn
old used for used read loved doll
arms on your arms if
that rates
don't wait wake take
never electric chair
maybe the dentist or the barber
or the wicker i am the moon master let doom
stet someone else's slimming already hare
eye forte there are those
fateful roses cutting all
the rabbit's noses off
and rats long as some
river hopeful creeks
everywhere since there is nowhere
they are not they are the godly
rats first wash the noses
in creeks then
white some returned to they
begin a berry-like eat revolving
it round so no two bites
fight with one another this is
the way to found a town
bury the distance stretcher sniffer here
and a rat eye so salt
with mourning doves' denials
of hero zero zero there their
unsure of bottoms stranger ranger weird wade

in what we would have head first
as to have drawn all distant
nearer here now now

when sky rips
the sky's everything so nothing
so vowel in a consonant kangaroo
so nothing rips the ground
then new frogs sing
for love from torn by zero all
every poem should sound that fretted ooh waa
not your idea of penury nor joy joe? then ta ta my ten
galleon tipped and shut the old creakin tree thing
tree never wood huff that's all on the hinge
all the soldiers unloading all the guns and rain
fakin headwaters of window's invention
me and my little spurting brim just before
end all war at the door
will have to do for city gate
where all great gestures by
flocks of birds absorb rain's
little lid shelved perts and ffts
claim is close to
milk upchucked by baby
mama no rag used to be a curtain
in smoker motel necessary
that sprite spout mite bee reuse friendly
for that child knows no sour
what she sees adds up she sees
two foot in front of her
words die about three
remember the rope
the frogs throw for love
is on fire you that drum
neck like piano thumb and

pinkie spider sucker
on fire the throats
of grass not battle
green for love

30

goose
friend
future man
don't let me catch you
average air and average room
that blind
does debtor better than wend
those old whale bone blinds
cold closed of plastic now
nothing groves natural for square
eggs can't take heat over mother
unless it's mother's no heat no weight
pillowcase without the pillow
dream without head
coaxes urges
same shape different i can't explain say
a not quite warm cloud
hovers demands it go against her
it supersede her like her
love her remember her different
than she was
hawaii has nothing on alaska sort of thing
hot sand is cool but where are the piano key face wolves sort of ting
great omelet belly light
ottawa in a blender
window sob the diner unclean
don't you have
a little pride in having tweaked
your own system of trusses for your old
mewling pains i am tramping
cloth for show dachshunds

torn but so goes the town
in my dreams don't let this be
ohh 2:12 pm
mmmm spinnaker dell
it's yours though
i mark your spine
straining fruit flies
from sweet vermouth
in the early afternoon window
garbaged with darker like a bear
with an itch against a birch
the word not the leprous tree

31

autumn's genial autisms mm in thick
dada dove country
star-birthed jars
dove's coyote
all glistered cistern sybilline
hmm genie i'll
yearling isle sapling eye gatlin pride
talkin walkin caught hot fridges
run for rim rime rhyme
and peas one money tree
dough make it a half hey
hey coconut love what i've seemed
need not sink in
the soft milked
milled by wind
eats of the eyes
stringy white
give name neigh skate lay quite skint

32

go down around in the call
mouth tongue faced without teeth
spiral stair held up there
wit dead kid whisper old kind supper
that's time and ignorance for you
we found we left table long enough
not to recognize one leg
on that outfit sat to a plate of stones
the pretty one has to show
her fair cheek on plates
of road says i am tired fez
on a shutterbug shut your eyes
i feel i've cleaned the world
unseen a small
lightning feels shakespearean
if only he'd had guns to go on
though instant kapow awol antihero
is in a flash i suppose the labor and twisting
of swords sparks
and grunts left off my page is key
man pees as you gut him off page key

33

hardy red flesh har
night's big winner ohh owl spine
brighted by world
read work
plough talk ohh
telemarketer's asteroid ear
i seen you comet comma coma coming
short hairs drawing
alka seltzer ads of you
mine white cloth around
the perimeter interiors of
a copper helmet hum pin
half whistle suspect tooth
mm the bled and running
holler or sugar a hole home
of a wild creature hmm
chew on the other side half
yourself is shy maybe kinder
pain there sharp pea for jerking
sweets love old m arnold me cuz
that door's a guy with a gun other side of the door
and a long complicated idea
about population control all
along there in there chomping

young love is a knee blood
for beauty and its exquisite hesitancies
stat rash can't believe
the loved makes waste
in the can first i know of you
annul a knoll those quiet waters
only jesus could icefish in summer
event lists lisp in fire
i felt bad for the fire could not talk right
stone went off like a shot
they worked on my teeth with pig fat all night
i could breathe out a farm
but i could not hire the labor
they call 'em dirt farmers because
that's their tooth on back that ant
event ants carry only resized moon
shield herald of
turn it it says good night
you dapper rascal you
now don't ya ever flue flu flu
bird ohh to hear young love
making water in the bathroom
bout three hour fore dawn all the world's a library
don all the cold people are tiny needles and
every cloud's shoulder's your grandmother the librarian
mmm some shy thread piercer
rebinds soft porns to spines
under the coverlets of the holy books
neither sheer nor shrill it's all just
big tits shower scenes it's
every s save one in

house for snake spaghetti-ing over highway
hurry-rah that's oop that fine name
for the rattler we trained
to mou(s)e wall(s) (s)topped
having heart(s) again

35

friends when you are hungover
as bog water in a bag with a hole in it
and lands that hall is long one
job forever peel them thirty worm
gird apples with naught but your fingernails
skin in refusal of skin
see nail and skin love too much
saw there is no entrance
to the body there
sweet hurt
bird city

36

through the church nurse
your fingernails then
spit no don't you out
them just let door
false lashes typeset is
what a wood your vision doll
that's a sign dine
salted touches
anyway anyhow and they
hell of a helicopter down

37

back on the bridge again
back to water's rusts
and the stones' russets
rusty fur of sediment-like sentiment
honey slice thru time let's
remember how shirts smelled
wind thru apple tree trees and
the sky mashed stones holy tater hoe
tonal truck passes
under a load again and i press again
against the bearded metal of the bridge

38

all my little stain water clear optimisms all this life long
lesson of pitted but whole
tshirt taking tasting red rust
sunset soft brand line
no that sun don't flatline
that's just the bridge under weather forever
only one story ever told of the fleck sneezin bridge
bang and everybody no just him running
to the cracked car wheels still spun
some high whine from the engine
short bus in a kid cavalcade
still in spin remember to pull before
the final version and the radio maybe daa danana
that time of night when the river
of a black light shined and the smell
of gasoline just pure god pissing
oh oh look away vinyl liar leather
pliers might as well been bird
siding done of old mixed tapes we
passed around when words
were new and love was breathless love
ohh too too twi-heads chopped off
by that benign old bastard bridge a woman
and man he guessed had been in love
for least a week and the smell of that
god damn buck butchery and the heads
like sports balls that could talk
punted but that's no conciliation
of a loss guy wearin iron
socks and a squared chin scare
a hairpin heavy petting instant lose

grain grime grind the belly swallows squirting
skate rave knife nice sneeze
pickle your favorite spasm
ice fresh dill in her eyes boys
all virtue in as if
think r frost thought that back
when i was eight and memorizing
snowy evening and messing up
at harness bells shake
like every time why

oho the rust smells
of when the oar died
a crack like a homer
man pound for pound this river water
that's alright
nothing dies say
through a quick sandwich taste
good paint stir stick sure
and i press again against the murderer
thirty year later
dish rag docile
that water never
never could be steam
we're soap out centuries and
friction's in millennially
lamb ear over tap's
too hard tab or tacit lack's
too hard and or ladder rash
ain't gonna get you new war
word doing a word
puzzle in jail back when
bars were of wood
and all you'd needed
was a yawnin dragon
can't thank elan enough
again against that

40

pinch little vision mirrors
in the many lined craw of paws
moonwalker member me in meet the crayfish destine
it don't have eyes in the back of its head
honey i B'd geometry i know
what's proved by cray-
fish
the world warms softs us
the hands of the world around us
the have not worked soft hands of blown dust
and every dust bit bids it all
on that pillowcase covets a headcase
so sot gusts preen in
set sedge to id
sayeth cray slowly
turning color of the river
the color of the farms
once were 40 cow
and a hard to get all in one
picture catholic family
the two geese we'd named
for weather chasing
sister daughter
probably because bored or maybe
inveterate meanness
is in anything
meant to watch pinching anyway
at her diaper
white furious whites
this trans mish ending
with a one eye kitten

strange hair
up an aspen in the season
of blood then brown

41

cool cool hot net the metal shakes
like a face in a laugh
the truck gone the bridge rings
like a tooth ache and then
the holy silence of the bridge
from which to edge is to be born
into the river i am the bridge and the stone
slips distant in my inner mind
sew watered eye
fish like flags of flesh at home
in time i know to move
is hunger's quit and friends with hunger's tater
tell it on mole hill
baa eye wad wider these and those are
fast and selfish trees
plump out quick
on id is it that's rye

42

mmm long time remembering
the tug of the waters against my ankles
in the days before hairs
something like time is a rinsing thing
or star a alabaster start or
like a river i am always just begin
if how you approach things is clean
then poke this way along
up over the lane where
the creaking and the fans and the more
more belts watch
your fingers around them friend
behind the beautiful rocking
never will quite quit tip
this grace friend
you don't have to wait for what i am talking about
hug me out airy fear manure carts
throwing turkey tail of you know what
till the land stands green
them golfing radicals
dream and drool
pillow so heather in linnet
you could wring it and
satiate an birdie
for least one two moon

43

sang baby why
and baby please men
great tall wide wild thins of sandpaper
slotted into the steel dowels
of the stars turn faster
faster sound no sound
if the thing is smoking
leave her lay a little
you don't know how to handle
that thing when i was young
men swung axes at things
axe heads like water wader bird heads
man metal live trapped the sun
little platter
little hearts little heads
made by years for fish
and patience slammed slams
sun fish that's man speed
leaned on remade
stump is turtle in a day
the beautiful zip
of a bowl flipped over
protects nothing holds nothing feeds nothing
what falls slips
down the sides
saul

44

you and only you
know how to sing to
the skips we were corn
the radiation we were popcorned
children sweet children
propped selves on elbows
rapt and tense at the scary part
ahh movie tv shine whirling
a camp fire flushed
down a toilet
we were good so good
to stay that
still as stone photographed
as they
as they picked from us
an idle idol of salts
and shuddering green
have no idea were we good

45

you and only you
dust has feelings too
flip the end first gyre in
collider scooper why wait
what is a slow build but a craft
for dune sand in your eyes i have been these
seventeen years under a vaunted
sky waiting for the 430 bus at 445
palaver there i said it
palaver rue the day
what a one shrimp roux
the cliff dwelling one of these days
gonna fall over open
like a sandwich like a face
in a laugh eighty nine
rules she was owl she was a shut rhyme
with owl bible? the flowers did not fade
the flowers were fake
though many cats
grew to great boxers
there at fair rebound's meaty shore

46

some countries say you have been there
no one knows the flavors of your gasolines say you have been there
count yourself low key
eat your language with your eyes
county your states just don't count on yourself
abacus beads oiled
to sigh lens by regrettable misers
they bought out the nipples too
don't count on yourself
you breeze err bruise too easy you factory mold for
boats of violet towers you
tongued and grooved in
pine pine

47

the rabbit is rabbits are
and an road petroleum glue
echo the roads
field is no future for roads
still a man can't help but dream a way through here
wants for noses in his eyes the then
know this field is in number
terms of the way through
the numbers of mouse holes in old houses
the term is a german word
limitless thick lighter liar pa
no don't it
don't let drear dad dead the dreamy views
man glisten before you listen
and tooth before you uh huh another's
suitable for framings
there let you
cat a hash the rhyme from there
cuz man teetertotter's ass logic
for ex twenty more than two
ways through

48

been barfing green kneelers since the two doves proved
that wire ain't worth an all day sit
day is church night is a hell if
i am a helicopter goat
am eating my spinner
serious about waiting
like scissors
the surgeons forgot in
if i bend just right you can hear the shearers
singing to ewes how impossibly sad it is
transport equals moving lives?
what are we to think
that they just got up and did the same every day
no think fantastical mountains
and that dewy river
moving morning laminate lazy
through a flood plain
where the gators
cranky on too saltless a water plashing
are loving or eating the frogs why else move?

49

37 by now keats Williams
charley patton are really
very dead maybe i've paid
in funeral two dollar bills
enough for my words to say
something grand of myself
but trailing off in volume at the end
to paddle myself live
live rich of eye and hand on the second growth ivy
shade of a passing hawk it's like a stage beard
on a cable pulled
across the planked ground it's like coffee
actually jumps if you stare it at right
that mine is goldless oh
show slow beard pen wool pencil filings firings well
nighttime well
one frog sings in clear
mood ring redder greener together
however the day goes
hits that cool of a searcher at and as
the wing and the wind and body crest
good dark touch'll just judge jug
hello higher bellow weather
clean breeze cleaning service sir vice sire
or teleprompt orgasm ash
ain't just for guns anymore o all over
my why all this my
our our now naturalized skin

50

there they all sleep
their middles thick
as with babies of
burnt ex deer
and the ash there
of the cooking fire
sunk like an old beard
the tragedian fondles
in his empty room
looks around no one
slips it up sturdy
against his unshaven chin
it's the little things
the hairs that hold it
in place wisp purrs
turn up the mic
to no one joy dumb
or joy or dumb
the birds the walls
the backstroking sill flies
the sills painted
white to give lipless
the faces of the walls
the tints of factory eggs
mercilessness in
hosed down steels
express for keeping
kept from creeping

51

we want the dog
for scarp sense
built blind debt deaf no hot
alphabetical nose
no the largeness mind
testifies to a
beguiled world
and that
not being able to
sense it
all we do is brood about it
want the dog
because straightness
is a guarantee every so
often of corners
off corners
is that a shadow
of a body closer closing
or leak of smoke
in the basement boys
washed in opium
o the dog solves
the meat a little time ago
the meats of their smoked up eyes glassed
as milk held on spoons spells
the cob ceiling you can
grab at that web but
down'll come the paint and old
tremble bunny morning me
hairs sleep
neck back to sleep

like good little campers
under a protean why
good boy

52

for every rabbit an owl
unglues the lanterns
of its eyes and leaning
from a high pine
fall and catch and down and rise and in
that time it's like
hearing an ambulance you pinch yourself
in the night the pain
ain't ate me
make fingers
like bird face in the night
the ambulance in morning
rotten apples
they must have had barn paint left
over for a corner touch up
with the point at the corner of the stiff wide brush
rotten apples
pucker to spit a barfight tooth
puck on the pines and it
wasn't me

53

and came the satanic train toy top
or god got booked finally and this is
his thumbprint bumping everything off
the poor won't have no light for a long time
move on move on
the rich and middle write poems about it
go to therapy about the train
song of death song of death song of death
unn the poems craw around
like a dog with no eyes
how the metal
went water mental in the wind and
they all were sucked out live in
pieces in georgia people keep telling me
ditch birds ain't people yeah right
right

54

you and only you
ware damaged is for free
all you have to do is haul it away
these days there are men
probably three by two
twangs of unsettled waistbands
that ringworm's a rare itch man
waiting on your everything
take it unsorted no problems
o though so holier soar
i want to
on the undigested tin of colanders into
the solar far roar just as
quiet as stone mud
in the gut of that thing world's quietest
instance of digestion them worms burn
past the local won't let rider ride horizon
razors all
hangers on
the black heat of beyond
ear hole of a star
makes you wanna slap a donkey
favorite favor down
saccharine we engineer
time sweet time
ain't got back again

55

ooh which is worse
the fox in the night
flaming robe
scratch scratch
turtle egg face fox first thing you learn
in painting is yellow and red don't mix
it'll take you back there
in a squalid squad car
or this walk that dog pees right there
in turtle dream soft
lower dirt is finer that's the bottom line
so
so is it
the fox tail low in tall grass
and licking his eggy chops like the sound
of the wind nosing in grass or old faithful
for whom each softness needs be
named old faithful

56

every morning i am thinking of how the night
stays until middle morning and
the guest divines the dinner
from scents off the yawns of the host
how an empty bottle rolls sounds
like the sands of time
picked up dirt as they went
opposed to weathering grow giant
the bowling balls of time in the temperatures of metal
and dew the guest turning
least eight of turn and wrinkled tine on the walk
home see that the left house still stands
now the light and yet and now it's out
window old radio for body window
i miss a lot of people
or myself
how i was
when they tell you how they're doing
cease chew
even the sound of breakfast in your head
could deny
the sitter the role of dancer
bed head
ben your cat is an hundred
in human and doin fine
bed head heed

57

junk is anything can't carry its own
pigeons fucking in fresh plant field
i am running
in secret cities we don't hear
we move i am saying
it's better to die yelling
in a field the cheapo butter dandelions
did this to me
i love the wind
would not bet on it the bit in it
belongs to dogs named for horses
hay burn my dogs proposing
fast dug graves
shovelfuls
whisking in

58

careful i enjoy darkness
most ink favorers do
so something brighter like healthy gums
pink shower curtain
a plastic one
gliding along behind a big boat in the ocean
gonna catch me a thousand underarms
right square in the no get away cheek
for there lie the bibles and
burbles babbles and towering
bubble climb of what mouths did
in the light and in lit dark
but mouths do nothing without hands
and hands are only fish
upon the waters of the mind
and no water hasn't current save
puddles and springless ponds and puddles
are only the past tense of driving rain
and anything past is now when spoken
so i think we have sufficiently
updated puddle ponds are for looking at
the message is relax or
easy to recognize on
country people they stink
dog is optional for knowing that

59

here's a love poem for s
watch out or i will tell how you feel
this morning massachusetts is so wide
shaky maybe public transportation forever
is the idea for the tattoo you'll never
sitting there
hands little sleeping wild animals
listen can't whistle that's a human
learned thing from birds and another
thing humans are trees and
no tree ever lived never had a nest
a nest is broken shit
some sharing singer bore in round
for another round of mmhmm haa haa
such is the promise of the stretch marked sky
all i am saying is there's a lot of sweet
soft song alive in brokenness in all of us
so mute wee hands maybe sun doused baby
bison maybe have legs for foraging for
eight ten nutrient rich flowers and so all that
dakota et cetera half eaten by your milk lap i would
take my socks off and and you could stick them on
your hands could rapture those zeroes
riding with do sock puppet plains cows
in search of dew drop daises again
when they bite down the dowdy flowers say
molar cholera came and boiled the plates?
ooh sing it all bust lip broken with me now zeroes
to ones and then you'd thumb them emblems
of docility old drift oh down unto the buttes
your beautiful kneecaps nuclear

plant dome caps storin story of snowy
wolf crouched next natural
apple afterbirth lamb both a little
blind harpsichordist both a little shy unsure
of what to happen to by a e smith with touch ups
and touche frowsy blossoms courtesy
praline of praline tasty snow

60

bye bye traffic in ghost type
the second hand has two gears
whisker pick and plangent
ohh wish
to sound one solid thing
twiddle boys just ain't an option
the bit hang
pest anapest if
deflection of a touch
is a declension's wreck then trust in something
a gun
without a soldier's same thing
but a sultan's sword's bowed because
we fight with ourselves
in the main
you must wheat this corn world
spit in the rain to get to him
only to deny him

61

kicked a carp
to a compact constable machine
rewind waterfall
all knee tippy skiff
ah roar
o the shell eyes of surprise
mm lonely abalone
hmm abilene mustard green
though under there the beauties bathe

62

darling cutting
all the trees in alabama
all at once now out-
side my window crazy
throaty chainsaw ha
haw hackled hackneyed
ain't no acne of smoke
swoon and bode and bad bowtie
boas on the leatherface
nape of aubade a bum a saint
a bomb a ray
curves curds by dint of worldly
like a tracer or a pill
the gravitational ends
the bride's split ends
the just out of jail peering
in through the bonds office
through a wreath hung against
giving no one
there buddy they are sleeping off
walker you paid for
at the lock up
but how saw gas scent hounds
the rabbits of yesteryear
corn stub's poor thwart
former den dog know no mind
is all legging nose and closing
forgive the dog the foaming
teeth nothing no one needs forgiving
only let us live in a lather and
what the hell wish me fast hole

now or i am sugar darkly sweetly
penned some sickly fog night punky
ohhh fallen fruit can't fall
farther than fair ground fat lie hoo
hoo how bout i
bird my rabbit and gone

adult compost

honest the cork cast no light

and then the one rooster opens

a fire eye and i quote stirs

figures no dawn folds again

into his rough it russet traveling share

probably a rabbit like an arthritic wave

in the green sea of the dog's dreaming mind

and i

why i float like a god

through the dampish linoleum

last seen producing a linoleum texture potato chip

from the chilly glow therein

maybe the real church is learning

not to hate folks with different

metabolisms than you and sweet

is the art of listening practiced

in the art of killing ghost i are

bitter bees the broken

elbows smoke

in their minds the guns pointing

downwards trained

on the dead holding up

the living while the bad men

is it true you can tell the crime

by just looking?

wild the see the snakes sleep in great big twister balls on

winter's

unders and

autumn forever fast food heart men there

always there hunting any little

old sheet of metal color ruined water

in the woods they will with a special stick

lift the edges of that

look long for the hiss hole

our foreheads wider

than ten tools molten

in a steel hell fire

i like that molted

winks at wings of fire

built not to forget

how quiet it gets in a forger's workroom

bubble and agonize

isinglass on an agate

smell of spring

green as a wound aired

soil crush

rest in the knowing

that's a bad add

knowing drives us mad egg

no the bones never cease their muttering

hush the sound of leaves

loaned from the bones shouted down

to soil you touch they are

the new of no feel

don't be vegetable designed for travel

don't sweaty tshirt flesh

twisted by twirling

to pop at a neighborhood menace

just like you to take the head off a chicken

oooh it all adds up to how many

times your heart clucks swallows knocks

in a minute and how hard

be surprised

but as through donation sunglasses

you decide when you let the smoke

from your nostrils fall

ghost getting into a pair of nylons

poison factory smoke sneaks

the dogs of night

all across the south ooh i need you

your killer mouth greens leaves

yesterday's road a coyote

what quiet must come to his cold wet nose

must be like lying awake at night in a large

city try new york it's late

and you are listening to the dial tone

everywhere is red and white light

and you are listening to the dial tone

back when there was a dial tone and

i can imagine the inventor of the dial tone

was like make it sound like a humming lizard

for many are the done wrong

and this'll be their algae elegiac theme song

without the heart to hang up

your nose in the glass case put

dwell with eye a little isle little

road for wild things a hang up

nothing to smell of on some bound

past the trees

lush tops

thin trunks

forever of fish bone

is the woods

and the woods will loco taco tackle you

out pattern this despite

the claims of the with-it crows

stick a noise on your foot

long the highway

black plastic sacks

tremble in the forever

evening gloaming summer light

weight all along the hip spin

pivot and throw them

free men chucking square bales

onto flatbeds

twang of bed bug bites

along chafes chafed

waistline kicking at a stone never did

never lick of harm

was just being mister stone

just sitting there

it's a funny sad

how hardness encourages abuse

okay follow fallow cola wind

oh

why you have eyes in your head balloon head rise rise

don't smile somebody said your teeth were screwy

plus this wind how many birds shat in

or sang same thing again again in and that's too sweet

you don't have all the money in the world

you need to date a dentist

leans into you

with her knee right there on your rye stomach

paints with her knee on your bell

logo for ocean

that's one fine teal wheel and

wheels and water don't mix

sweet candy head orpheus

through as though gone fishing for wings

with wings but no wing bites on a wing

way to catch a leper is with a limper fixture sprat

way to catch an angel is to lampshade out the window

your best garlic sigh way to snag a wing is lie you leased

the ice factory to the cup factory

oh no? well then how come now no one

doesn't have a wet upper lip from all time cool heel

drop the h and you lonely onus parade honey sippin

polka dots and cool that's sipping do

that thing with your pony

whale again

there again with the chasing

your own bag of snake intestine

beer and cakes bent double

that machined batter got me in the gut

wool on skin of the far crows scratching out

a little burro puke saw on the wind

on the wind it ain't that good but say it again on the wind

all the seeds plunge

like lovers kept from each other

by blind cruel mothers

plunge into the other's body

or the starving man the body

of the fire charmed squirrel

can i meet you where

the carvers

unknowing

deep in meat

lined the joints

the grooved bone won

worn by blade

little chalk road leave the bled lip teachers out of this

milk can for a chair

easy fall it's all in the legs

a cad dough winter

recant wee spring rant

feeling bad gets old quick now

little ferrous tint minus sign

we word the world sweet grinds

to keep our teeth

from stretching long

as fish never come out

of darkest cave

telescope lip squinty pursy star

she could work in the garden

three kids on her

and the fourth in her

the deer here

there everywhere

higher than they have to

with a little leg kick and pharaoh's

smoke-like glide before the meat and ten

hundred wet clean through socks

in the cyclones of their hollow bones

suck them back to earth in slaking stun

stunted fived by no no white why

this the force of the ghost fences

the animal forever navigating

the sense of former human meats

butcher beef a piece of a land

the wilds shout

yes but then move on

it's a saturday monday let's get drunk

let's let a pair of swirl eyes

pinwheel meets up with whirlpool

lollipop what can i learn from you

except that sweetness ends in blindness

nets

around planet stars through which

swish moonshine wine

sagacious organ

in a silo sad vetch gas believe i

sigh a killing rah and made love

for fourteen years no children

cried we cried out

as children do before words

in the words of gods

in the stuff of words

without hammering 'em closed and yes

yes a pain right

fight love

the clock sounds like a thousand people far

away walking

what is it in an antler

that shivers men

is it carpenters

and the crookedness pisses us off

i refer to them syrup makin days

if you haven't been in one of those dorito for breakfast dorado schools

you would not know

i did learn biting from her good

god shh she raked the leaves

the wind tipped timbers

them root gnarl in exes on the grates

where the street corner curb

high as a wall for drunken atavistic loafers came

gonna wear you out with the particulars

because there are too many of us

with the same name fell like a what

name like a grate on a name

street street street i guess that's a town

floods every time it rains

keep a mattress in the elms and shut up on sundays

two bird fart a country vay cay makes these days

regret gets old quick now i find i love a broadness of face

and the days alone

in car with other

wind from speed in

between seasons and towns

the possibility of permanent damage

like dogs let us not

stick our faces let us

stage an side approach

your own footfall

on little stone dirt someone trying

to light matches in a wind

muttering oaths

against reproduction

and it was a home steppers be damned

peace lightning mr rodney the dog who ate a whole lot of tennis ball

fluff and then a needle and then birthed shat

the needle in a cocoon of yellow came

the needle having learned what there is of dog

no it was as dumb as it was when it went in

see a needle's too purposeful to stand

accused of learning's little bridge mints

pivots and corrections now that was a lucky dog

that's no fun for wrong place wrong time spider

falling through the cement mixer meadow

station one in sheep gut and

inside spider one last flywing

crying itself to sleep

silver thimble of warm milk on the rained sill

pitiful little fly couldn't afford a bedside mesa

see the shine's so shine

as to sound the sounds culled squeak and sweet

when stairs turn to water

boys when stairs turn water

oooh we'll swim to sweep

we must as dogs do

walk side to side and cut our eyes

the charcoal so called chainsaws begin

now there is nowhere the eye can't go

my grandpa and i barking at one another

from screened in porches

across yards covered in bone

and broken toys in my blood

one

eye of a farmer and one of a slicker

i am by definition lost

and the trees come down off the trees

and the calcium climbs

down off of the bone

that eyelash ain't no tree

she's the lumberjack of my saturday monday blink

she's my kind of hen

the remember when hen

feathers but she won't sky

cluck but she won't time me sweet

stuff the suitcase you didn't pack

enough to need to roll oooh whee

she's all future we'll gather for cake lately

i want this

to scare your heart clean to

scare clean your heart a little

my name won't always be

night bus to nowhere

where the woods leave off

and the wet often in the sky

like a slug slime

all that sex wet on a laundromat pointless dime

woods all black and back there

wooing happened with a knife that shot bull whips

they were unfolding cars

like love letters over where no grass

it was a life size replica

of an aztec ball court

they only touched the ball

with their hips

you could steer the wheel

to move the bruising ball

we both peering

like a double moon

at the priests had never cut their hair

was matted and relatively crazy

i could not take my mind off

a goddess with a ceramic chalice

full of human blood? did not

keep her from applauding

and the contents

giggling over the unmoved rim

and the quadruple five stain vanishing

name in 'nother name

love is a squirt gun hold up

fuck you i was trying to spray

that food spot off your shirt

the pigeons everyone writes it same insane clap

off towards abandoned silo

to sit and shit and turn to thinking

of nothing only they see

and do not see

the oil of a finger

is a cyclone

tree of stone

don't you know my little dears

the ash of vesuvius

was once so much burning

earth blood

all british

precision knife and fork

through the singlet of a decorous pea

in a pubic hair of flowers

of flowers

shuts his eyes

licks the pan

day old pig cream

still a castle wall

yank hair dream

older love i forgive you for

not heating up the cast iron

therefore these mop bucket onions

maybe i might before

breeze before i squeeze on

past that can door i might work

one more word on the cross

or hell

tour the yard every spring

some old new thing rising

like a promise up the throat

of a drinker

knuckle some ash to that child

let roar him

what i am sweating smells of festal

therefore the parlor

no one goes in

and dip your nose into your shirt

like you are opting out of getting born

hide a little in what happened

remember you are only

tenant of hands jerk

i didn't overhear it

nobody kept rain in mouth

all day until it was 97 degrees

said shut your eyes but hated

the shortness of a u so my my

shoot your eye with a car crash

but sweety oh sweety i am the carless badger

just this little nothing ever me

lie i got five car smashed

and then i laid down and she

put that unworded

unphrased rain right on my vision almonds

is this what you do? with your free time? porn

think of the one that will not live

but reads of life

until the mind is

as wealthy in worlds

as a goat is of tin cans

nailed with his tether

by the fool

to sandy soil by the burn pit

that and naked pictures

revolve in the system of the goat

think of how uncareful roughly

hewn lids are with images

think of how uncareful readers

are with people

when people are animals

think of the gloves we used to wear

for driving think of this cow

jawing on relatively flat terrain

think of the ladies riding the cows and ducking under

certain mossy limbs

and the mossed vines lifting off the limbs in a wind

like snakes dreaming of party streamers

think of the falling mouse satisfied snakes

think of how no mouse can last

hurry think glue tree nail songs

kept the snakes to their hollows

because even a snake admires rehearsal of feeling

of the straightness with which they rode

the cows a straightness everywhere mourned

call it the curse of the chair think how

careful the cow think how tender foot

think of all the cow knows of

one blade of grass having known it

seven ways whereas our lives

are so much a knowing of

two or three fashionings

of a person i feel a chair blues coming on

the snake song went with them

into the ground

the best medicine is carrying chairs

i am testament to this

there was that tender ginger

fucking with the weft of time

eerie superior mothered one

my short land saint hesitant in

dust carcass fish prize

it's just for picturing

it was a good fight i will always

have the electric no

yes this fit river

my every puff out points the unway

what good is morning

to a factory sleeve?

but still as the ditch dictum mourns

the cave stillll i van with the romance of a boy

and a girl biking home with river in ear

putting cotton torch bunk ash on all the crows'

false wire tappings try and tell you

what you are hearing when you are seeing silent black

the highway late and trans

lush did it or wine did him

in the morning out on the porch

needs fixing

has needed for oh hell

if you don't go through

then you will go along

maybe they cock their heads

and spanking at their heads

mama dada and the kid

you learn all the fine little things

so to say

of a transportation nightmare so to say

that's what they are trying to do i can see it now

knock the go out

i will not will not will not will not will not i will not i

will not

love anyone speaks dead

nor ahead i will love the one

who speaks as it is happening

all weekend i been hearin about

daddy long legs poison and deep fried beer

friends get beautiful wrecked by a vision

get shocked

your heart punch your neck

jump back

break fence

get young gusts

don't let news fool you

it's always the worst almost now

whyy yes it is good to tell

never tire telling of the tractor stuck we tried pull it

with the truck i gunned it

the chain snapped and flew

a snake in a snatching mood

and i instinctual

on the candy wrapper floorboard

showered in candy teeth of glass

as snapped chain

hungered round headrests

having whistled weird high so i could not hear

the fun the paid men

would have had stacking my head back on

the forgers of a pulse

their chains heading for

watches in pockets

some heirloom maybe

here they are standing over former sort of farmer smithy

one with my head one watches all the poor rest

ha ha look at the bunch of overgrown mud daubers

in science guess glasses

never read shakespeare

or read too much

one chewing wads of paper

down to the right white to pat in

as bridge for what neck stayed in that may field

stupid pure i don't have to ink the birds descending

you got that black okay

if everything is for hiding

i can't tell the former world of the robin

beak yellow that's so seed sure

but why the orange frontal

was a former time before the farmer

trying all a wild ripening always

and this the bird meant to mingle

with one day out from rot fruit

late last night they were coming for me

the men it was only

rain falling in twos

and then a whole sled of them unbathed with sledges

on fire no it was just my pigeons

in a slit cairn tum it was

the simple kid on a snow sled

down a dewed summer jack

it was just just passage of food jerking

through unimproved lane no path no pave

was an honest missed lake

and i

i was all new in the knowing

of myself and scolded me for plotting fear

in myself dental floss bridges boys pop

pop pine tar up over the label

oyyyy in 1983

can't i can't help but mage magi inn in these

teeth marks on wind

from your sneeze flamed

doll sneeze on me a river

a way

even just a little milked antler of la la light

to guy me out

out this my

dry dark

dark

dark

dark

dark old time probably

never was

as word will fuzz the world

cert certain certainly

ne'er star peach

never nair in a bullion for free

anything with cant

cannot mete horizon

canned meat hoar eye sun son

weak candle lead we

canary bozo pray

foot rot bunker reborn fun rut for kids

after the war no such

thing as after the war

only one backward glance

as next boom somewhere

licks the ice cream cone cup

all that suction and tendon

in shoulder shifty

stick your head out down

fair vanilla animal

through the cleaver heavy fogs

towards the fair for

next for the next sought saws choirs reeds

require no see eye blah

blah blot blah to

route clean one three

yeah lines like and

and for the dust

of startled wells to start

the dig gain

and deeper find

water's just gun and fence metal melted down

and stone is clap keeping things from you

and all the endless bully birds

all bomb about the blame game

crave congress crave

way they beat you up with

a school tray over the head

of love junk musics sing it hollow tub

the wind makes say lube or dud or

dude a gruesome grouts a groove

somewhere near bruce

wisconsin on a swill shoal sheep farm

it's wind it's work will bleep us clean

epilogue

*

back before the new asshole father with an anger management issue
after they shipped the other father who was gentle and kind talked like
he was talking about a silent movie on a telephone on the radio in a
silent movie they shipped him up by the Polish for he was boning his
secretary who would one day blow herself away with his elk hunting
rifle back before father anger would not let my mother take commu-
nion for the divorces she would read sometimes a passage like an angel
and always bring me back people ask me no a poem raps a miser's
knuckle on the bridge of the nose or more sensitive the eye about
what i remember when going to bed an automatic predream of small
boulders that pushed against my small palms but with the weight of
real boulders impossible skin fail 'gainst such heavies and then maybe
i could not sleep for a little while while the worry visited with me like
the father heavy of snuff and brandy the sickbed of the unbeliever you
can do that sort of thing when you are talking over praying for your-
self really heavy of corned beef light of toast heavy margarine in the
days before real butter was advertised with merry very confident best
neighbor i ever had would jump your car but otherwise stay out of
your hair glee cows again

**

and i remember alone in the woods the chickadee my only friend
don't laugh the chickadee did though nature didn't deny me and my
mother back at our pew because i was too small to take it she would
have saved a small piece in her mouth she must have minced it around
the way later i was taught not to and then she'd produce the jesus toast
a sail of a fingernail after a whale of a tropical storm she'd hold it out
to me on the pad of her right index maybe she'd drunk the stormy
blood of christ too yes she had also there were indians in the library
and i felt right among them

***

i don't know how i got it off her because it clung but i did get and put
the little warm triangle like the bit of eggshell in the egg you curse in the
pan before the heat carries it over it's good for what it's good for there's
hard in soft et cetera and calcium mouth warm as the right and left
hands of lovers tangled pretty like two halves of a clam with a flashlight
flash all ghost flesh on the grass path to the river on a warm night why
i put flashlight in there my mother their wine way may into june all
day the next minutes church you do count time ticket i had worked for
years and i was on vacation and i was the guy sold you the machine that
drilled the holes in bowling balls special vacuum too to get at that drill
dust is finer than a silk kerchief thrown up eighty times by a cow green
naked women on a private movie channel in a rented room so near the
big wash you could hear the salt stun glass bay i had had the name for
since second grade run through ropes of water happy and so far from
thinking southern cali had hip watered lawns in 1980 it is crazy but
they were right here closer than i behave like pawpaw his worsts every
day as in flip off the driver and squeal stud man that water must hurt
good ropes of cold run toe run kid run to feel the world's something you
balance on not old guy checks his bank count every half a dozen they
their small smoke head hands kept pushing down sweet old hissing down
invisible straw hula skirts kept riding up to juicy too twenty two hands
cupped inverse tulip gentle lithe pulling smoke out of skin kept pushing
down legs down off their legs unless their knee thigh lest all of it crawled
up on their hips and they'd of had to walk on faces by wink love lovingly
because happy and running and laughing and naked and green

AFTERWORD:

like a dangerous splinter in the heart: on abe smith's greatness

by Joyelle McSweeney

In cloven signature stray
come now with a voice
like a coffee table and steer
a picaresque with me

People ask where are the great poets of today—the poets of ambition, genius, music, devotion we associate with those who 'were truly great', whose work reflects an evident tutelage not in MFA programs but in the singing school Yeats' hymned in "Sailing to Byzantium". There's a lot wrong with this question, for ours may be an age of scattered greatness, greatness like disjecta membra—a stray bullet, runoff from a superfund site, shrapnel from an IED or shards from a vessel smashed up in the National Museum of Iraq. The bullet sinks, the carcinogen waits, the fragments split and divide; now greatness is nearly worthless, does not look like greatness anymore; it seeps or flies; it settles in bodies alive and dead; some is lost forever; some animates; some is digested; some lodges in the flesh or makes its way to the heart; an insult to the system; it causes fibrillation; or bursts the heart; and from this catastrophe death or rage or poetry is released.

this heart lotus clock galosh
this head this crisp vie 'zine sail

Abraham Smith carries greatness like a dangerous splinter in the lining of the heart. He carries it like a poison drunk up in infancy, a bone shard that traveled from a smashed rib or a flint of exploitation that was planted there by a bad friend or a wasted economic system. Yet music pours from Smith like blood, cheap wine, car-radio and birdsong. Abe is an ecstatic, standing outside himself and singing to himself, the whole pulling-apart yet encapsulated pageant of Keats' Nightingale played out in the person of one poet. Abe is the bird and the poet, the one who flies and the one who stays, the one who knows the world and the one who knows only sonority. This irreducibility is what gives his poems their acute beauty, driving joy and unplaceable sadness.

and I remember alone in the woods the chickadee my only friend don't laugh the chickadee did though nature didn't deny me and my mother back in our pew

Abe also carries with him a sense of the world formed during a poor childhood in Ladysmith, WI, which the benefits of an adult perspective have rendered more and more permanently indicative of how the world really works. Life is hard, resources are few, poverty is so flattening as to be also comic, delight is also comically intense and brief, Nature is a sure consolation, and possibly something more, an indicator of another world, adjacent to the human world yet only appearing in the corner of vision, possibly only an error in perception, possibly a lit up celestial park. Thus the familiar species—rabbits, dogs, sheep, frogs, owls, non-specified fish and birds—which appeared to Smith as a child remain in his field of vision, crashing the poems, crashing back into the frame and wheeling off again, resolving individual poems and keeping the project itself leaning forward into nextness, the next line, the next image, the next song. It is this inclination that gives the poems their deceptive lightness, their surprising juxtapositions, their forward tilt.

I am a helicopter goat
am eating my spinner
serious about waiting
like scissors
the surgeons forgot in
if I bend just right you can hear the shearers
singing to ewes how impossibly sad it is

In this passage each new line presents a bladed phrase which 'spins' the sense of the poem around—the goat has swallowed a helicopter, the "I" has somehow swallowed both and assumed the goat's position, the i-goat also contains a dangerous second set of blades, "scissors/ the surgeons forgot in". The surgery image, like the implanted helicopter, calls up the veniality of the human, who cannot only help but must always also hurt, even when making a lovely, soothing, predatory song—"the shearers/singing to ewes". In this passage we see the pastoral, a classic mode of poetry, superimposed on the 21st century plight of permanent warfare, at once technologically enhanced and, in its damage to bodies of any species, analog. Smith's song may be 'impossibly sad' but it proceeds by a series of skips and jumps at once unanticipatable and inevitable, and there is delight and even joy in these leaps. This, I think, is Smith's particular greatness. The beautiful is never divorced from the painful, the natural from the human, the eternal from the contemporary. Leaping from line to line, he registers life's outrageous, hardly bearable ongoingness.

what kept me
from shooting myself

when i was ten
was going to the river bridge
fish like flags that's all
all i have ever had
to say
fish like flags and i probably stolid
that from v woolf
sometimes comfortable
with the current sometimes advancing on it
like life

w/ especial thanks: for the inspirations, terrorisms, kindnesses, & love

richard smith; edward meisegeier; meggan meisegeier; the hawks' highland gang: angus, pip, and rosy; erin kavanagh; patrick kavanagh; pamela carazo; emily wittman; jessica mcbride; ashley chambers; monica detra; beth harrison; scott mcwaters; ashley mcwaters; bob davenport; jane detra davenport; john wingard; casey fagan; bill pfalzgraf; joel brouwer; david floyd; aubrey lenahan; shelly taylor; joanna lehan; edward zeizel; joshua marie wilkinson; eric parker; jason busse; shawn averkamp; susan brennan; steve timm; shrode hargis; tim croft; john pursley; k.c. vick; emily conner; samuel gray; kristen schiele; jenny gropp hess; tim earley; patti white; brent hendricks; kate bernheimer; carol eichelberger; jean mills; jessica peterson; nathan parker; joyelle mcsweeney; johannes goransson; and jerry goldberg

ABRAHAM SMITH

Abraham Smith hails from Ladysmith, Wisconsin. His previous poetry collections—*Whim Man Mammon* and *Hank*—are also available from Action Books. Smith summer-farmhands at Hawks' Highland Farm; winters as Instructor of English at University of Alabama.